T0280060

IMAGES
of America

JIM GATCHELL
MEMORIAL MUSEUM

IMAGES
of America

JIM GATCHELL
MEMORIAL MUSEUM

Jennifer Romanoski and the
Jim Gatchell Memorial Museum

ARCADIA
PUBLISHING

Published by Arcadia Publishing
Charleston, South Carolina

Printed in the United States of America

Library of Congress Control Number: 2022948608

For all general information, please contact Arcadia Publishing:
Telephone 843-853-2070
Fax 843-853-0044
E-mail sales@arcadiapublishing.com
For customer service and orders:
Toll-Free 1-888-313-2665

Visit us on the Internet at www.arcadiapublishing.com

CONTENTS

ACKNOWLEDGMENTS

The author would like to thank everyone within the Jim Gatchell Memorial Museum who supported her efforts to present the legacy of Jim Gatchell and his role in the establishment of the museum. She would like to thank her editor Stacia Bannerman for guiding her through this publishing endeavor. She would also like to thank her parents, Steven and Margaret Romanoski.

Most of the photographs in this publication were obtained from the collections and records of the Jim Gatchell Memorial Museum. As such, all photographs appear courtesy of the Jim Gatchell Memorial Museum unless otherwise noted.

All historical information provided in this publication owes much to Gil Bollinger's *Jim Gatchell: The Man and the Museum*, and research conducted by staff and volunteers of the Jim Gatchell Memorial Museum. All information has been reviewed for accuracy by the Jim Gatchell Memorial Museum publications committee, consisting of Sharon Miller, Nancy Pedro, Brucie Connell, and Sylvia Bruner.

INTRODUCTION

Museums are key to a community's identity, history, and economic well-being. According to the American Alliance of Museums (AAM):

- Museums support more than 726,000 American jobs.
- Museums contribute $50 billion to the US economy each year.
- 76 percent of all US leisure travelers participate in cultural or heritage activities such as visiting museums, and spend 60 percent more on average than other leisure travelers.
- Museums generate more than $12 billion in tax revenue, one third of it going to state and local governments.
- Museums and other nonprofit cultural organizations return more than $5 in tax revenues for every $1 they receive in funding from all levels of government.

Museums in small towns like Buffalo, Wyoming, bring visitors to a community and play a large role in recreation and tourism dollars. This book about the Jim Gatchell Memorial Museum highlights the trials and triumphs that small-sized museums (with a budget under $250,000) can experience across the United States. Some of these trials can include funding and staffing issues, while triumphs can come in the form of hiring the right people at the right time, enhanced community presence through programs and events, and the goal of national accreditation.

The Jim Gatchell Memorial Museum is a regional history museum at the foot of the Bighorn National Forest in Wyoming along Interstates 90 and 25 and US Route 16, within Johnson County and the Powder River country, which extends from the Platte River north to the Yellowstone River and from the Bighorn Mountains east to the Black Hills of South Dakota. This region was the last great hunting grounds of the Northern Plains Indians: the Sioux, Crow, Northern Cheyenne, Arapaho, and Shoshone. The discovery of gold in western Montana led directly to the establishment of the Bozeman Trail through this region. The resulting migrations went through the heart of the Plains Indians' prime hunting ground, with a negative effect on the land and game animals. This conflict led to the Plains Indian wars of the 1860s and 1870s such as the Wagon Box Fight, Fetterman Fight, Dull Knife Battle, and other skirmishes just outside of Buffalo. By the end of the Indian wars in the 1890s, Native Americans were on reservations and military forts and emigrant trails gave way to homesteaders, cattle barons, and businesspeople who created early western communities such as Buffalo.

Established in 1957, the nucleus of the museum's collection came from pharmacist Theodore James "Jim" Gatchell. When Gatchell opened the Buffalo Pharmacy (later the Gatchell Drug Store) in 1900, it had an immediate effect on the Johnson County community, bringing in people from across the region. Gatchell enjoyed getting to know his customers and befriended many. Famous Army scouts, cowboys, cattle barons, Native Americans, and lawmen all frequented the pharmacy, sharing their stories of life, work, and war with Gatchell.

Before arriving in Buffalo, Gatchell had grown up on a Lakota Sioux reservation and was fluent in the Lakota language. Because of this and his caring nature, he became a trusted friend of the region's Native Americans and was called a "medicine man." They brought him many gifts through the years, including firearms, war bonnets, tools, medicine bags, bows, arrows, and clothing. As word about these gifts spread, friends and acquaintances began donating mementos of historic people, places, and events from Johnson County and the Powder River country. Gatchell collected during a time when many historical figures were still present, and battles and emigrant trails were still in recent memory. At the time of the pharmacy's opening, the region's local military post, Fort McKinney, had closed only five years prior in 1895. The Johnson County Cattle War, a pivotal event between cattle barons and independent homesteaders and ranchers, had occurred in 1892.

After Gatchell's death in 1954, his family generously donated his vast collection to the people of Johnson County with the provision that a museum be built to house it. After three years of fundraising and planning, the museum was established in 1957. For the first few decades of the museum, it was only open during the summer months. The museum's current operation dates to the growth and development started in 1990 and continues into the second decade of the second millennium.

This book celebrates the life and legacy of Jim Gatchell. It focuses on how the Buffalo community united and created the Jim Gatchell Memorial Museum, and its early decades. It reflects the fluid definition of what it meant to be a museum in the 1950s and its transition to a modern interpretive museum of the present day. The Jim Gatchell Memorial Museum started out as primarily a collecting museum, with most of its artifacts on display. Today, the museum collection contains over 42,000 artifacts, a very significant increase from Gatchell's original 1,200-plus objects. Thirty-nine museum treasures that are considered the highlights of the museum, as defined by visitors, staff, and community members, are showcased in the last chapter.

As museum staff and governing board members educated themselves on the many different aspects that make up a museum, increasingly they felt that a good museum was made up of three components: collections, exhibits, and education. A museum needs artifacts to have a viable collection, and exhibits need artifacts to support a museum's objective. Like a three-legged stool, all provide equal support to fulfill a museum's purpose. Programs, both on-site and off-site, enhance and support exhibits within the museum building.

This book also includes a chapter on the progression of programs and events offered by the Jim Gatchell Memorial Museum. Educational programming was an area the museum was not focused on until it underwent accreditation with AAM in the 1990s. Staff and board members increasingly felt that the museum needed a full-time educator. That person by default is one of the most visible museum personnel. They are the chief promoter of a museum's mission and values through programming and events and help develop community collaborations. Program failures and triumphs are highlighted in this chapter. By the end of the book, readers will know who Jim Gatchell was and why we need to acknowledge his contribution to the community of Buffalo and the region.

One

JIM GATCHELL, THE MAN BEHIND THE MUSEUM

Jim Gatchell's father, Prince Albert Gatchell (right), was born in Maine in 1841. Historically, their surname was spelled "Getchell," but Jim's grandfather changed it. Prince enlisted in the 1st Maine Artillery in 1862 during the Civil War and achieved the rank of brevet major. He was with Gen. Ulysses S. Grant's army during the sieges of Richmond and Petersburg and was at Appomattox Court House during Gen. Robert E. Lee's surrender.

After passing the bar, Prince Albert Gatchell (second from right) moved his family to Wisconsin and practiced law for three years. He got into the newspaper business in Minnesota in 1873. The family moved to Dakota Territory, then to Nebraska and Wyoming Territory, where Prince purchased the *Sheridan Daily Journal*. In 1897, he started a new career in civic engagement, serving two terms as adjutant general of Wyoming.

Theodore James "Jim" Gatchell was born to Prince Albert and Hattie Ostrander Gatchell in Black River Falls, Wisconsin, in 1872. Jim's brothers were Albert, Prince, and Frank, and his sisters were Bessie and Daisy. Jim's formal education was sparse, and he was first employed in a department store in Lincoln, Nebraska. Later he worked for his father's newspaper in Sheridan, Wyoming, before continuing his pharmacy education at Edelman Drug Company.

During the Spanish-American War in 1898, the Wyoming National Guard Company C, 1st Wyoming Infantry, formed with volunteers from Sheridan and Johnson Counties. From this company, Jim Gatchell assisted in the formation of Troop E of the 2nd Volunteer Cavalry, which became known as "Torrey's Rough Riders." This photograph shows Torrey's cavalry in Jacksonville, Florida. The war ended while Gatchell was still in training.

Gatchell first achieved the rank of sergeant and was then commissioned as a second lieutenant in Troop E of the 2nd Volunteer Cavalry before the war ended. He continued to serve in the Wyoming National Guard and was promoted to first lieutenant in 1910. He stayed active in veterans' organizations for the remainder of his life. This photograph shows Gatchell in his Spanish–American War uniform.

Jim Gatchell and his family moved to Merna, Nebraska, in 1892, where he began his pharmacy apprenticeship. Moving to Sheridan, Wyoming, in 1894, Gatchell opened his first drug store in Big Horn in 1897. In 1900, the store was relocated to Buffalo and named the Buffalo Pharmacy before changing its name to the Gatchell Drug Store in 1917. It was located for most of its 88 years at 76 South Main Street. The February 22, 1900, issue of the *Buffalo Bulletin* mentioned that Gatchell had a partner for his relocated business that was going to be a combined jewelry and drug store. The partnership did not continue, as the May 24, 1900, issue declared: "The Buffalo Pharmacy is now open [and] ready for business, and the proprietor, T J. Gatchell, will treat everyone fairly." This photograph shows the original façade of the Buffalo Pharmacy with Gatchell in front of the door.

This photograph was taken shortly after Gatchell remodeled the interior and exterior of the store in 1941. He used the occasion to celebrate the 41st anniversary of being in business. He even received a congratulatory letter from Buffalo servicemen stationed at Camp Lewis, Washington. Modern visitors to Buffalo will easily recognize this location, as not much has changed on the exterior.

Every year, Gatchell had to renew his pharmacy license. His 1908 license was issued on January 7, 1908, and permitted him to "open and conduct a Pharmacy, Dispensary, Drugstore, Apothecary Shop, or Store, for the purpose of retailing, compounding or dispensing Drugs, Medicines, or Poisons" through the end of the year.

Prince Albert Gatchell was an accomplished musician, playing baritone saxophone for the first band in Clear Lake, Dakota Territory, in 1885. In 1902, he was the vocalist for the Buffalo Philharmonic Orchestra. Inheriting his father's musical talents, Jim studied violin and became accomplished enough that he was able to earn extra income with local orchestras and bands. This photograph shows a community band on the Johnson County Courthouse lawn.

Civic-minded Jim Gatchell sold tickets to various community events such as musicals, wrestling matches, and conventions at his store. In the early days of the Buffalo Pharmacy, Gatchell also sponsored one of the first baseball teams in Buffalo. The eight uniformed players and the two other boys in this photograph are unidentified.

This is the November 21, 1900, marriage portrait of Jim Gatchell and Ursula "Sula" Sackett. Sula, born in Culbertson, Nebraska, on December 2, 1877, moved with her family to Cheyenne, Wyoming Territory, in 1879. Later they moved to Little Goose Creek on the Bozeman Trail near the present site of Big Horn in October 1880. She earned her teaching certificate in 1897 from the Wyoming Collegiate Institute of Big Horn, graduating with her brother Carl Sackett as two of the four class members. She taught locally until her marriage. Sula Gatchell was active in civic and church organizations such as the Order of the Eastern Star, the local woman's study club Friends in Council, Pioneer Association of Sheridan and Johnson Counties, Old Settlers Association of Johnson County, Spanish–American War Veterans Auxiliary, and the Episcopal Church. She worked for many years alongside Jim at the Gatchell Drug Store.

Like his wife, Jim Gatchell was active in Buffalo's community life. He served in organizations such as the Spanish–American War Veterans, Johnson County Fair and Industrial Convention Committee, the Algonquin Club, the Fraternal Order of the Eagles, the Independent Order of Odd Fellows, and the Engine and Hose Volunteer Fire Company. In this 1900 photograph, Wilbur Holt (seated) and Carl Kube are wearing Engine and Hose Volunteer Fire Company uniforms.

As a firefighter, Gatchell was injured twice. In 1906, fifty men went into the Munkres Coal Mine (pictured) to construct temporary walls to isolate burning chambers. Many, including Gatchell, succumbed to the gases and had to be revived using artificial respiration. While fighting a fire in January 1911, Gatchell slipped from the roof of the Capitol Café and Grill, striking his head on the sidewalk and losing consciousness.

The line of merchandise offered at the Gatchell Drug Store was not typical of other stores. Gatchell offered all the standard drugstore items—prescriptions, drugs, patent medicines—as well as his own ointments and vitamins, along with toilet articles, perfumes, candies, books, stationery, cigars and cigarettes, greeting cards, and an ice-cream fountain service. Some store merchandise can be seen behind Gatchell (center) in November 1946.

Because Gatchell had veterinary training, he also offered livestock vaccines and animal medical and surgical supplies. Special animal prescriptions included "wire cut liniment" for horses and "maggot dope" for sheep. Non-pharmacy goods included paints, varnishes, phonographs, dolls, records, and leather goods. However, he did not stock tools, firearms, clothing, food, or household supplies. This photograph shows him at right inside the store with an unidentified man.

Jim Gatchell extended a line of credit to ranchers during the year and then billed them in the fall after they had shipped their calves. One time, in the 1930s, the Springer family incurred a large store bill due to a serious family illness. Cattle prices were very low, and ranchers were having a hard time making a living. When Elza Springer went to pay $250 toward his $500 bill, Gatchell told him, "You have had a lot of charges lately because of sickness in the family. There are many who owe me money, but don't try to pay their bills like you are doing now. You give me the $250 and your bill is paid in full." Above are cattle at the Hat Ranch; below are cowboys.

Gatchell is pictured with two pairs of glasses on his face, reading an issue of *The Billings Gazette* in his store. Gatchell had a soft spot for children and a special rapport with them. Many children were very comfortable in his presence. He was reported as not speaking "up" or "down" to them. Children even had their own small table with chairs in the soda fountain area. No child was refused an ice-cream cone, whether they had money or not. The ice cream was made in a small shed behind the store where a freezer was operated by a gasoline engine. When local children heard the engine's "chug-chugging" noise, they would come running because if they arrived before the cans of ice cream were put in the soda fountain to harden, they would be treated to a helping of soft ice cream.

The Gatchell Drug Store experienced many pivotal events over its long history. On June 11, 1912, a sudden cloudburst dropped up to six feet of water on Buffalo. Clear Creek flooded and detached the laundry building from the Occidental Hotel, lodging it against the Main Street Bridge. The water pressure and depth increased, causing the bridge to collapse. The surging water punched through walls and doors, lifted store floors several feet, and swept furniture and merchandise

into Main Street. The drugstore had 18 inches of water that left six inches of mud, and a cellar full of mud and water. Gatchell lost $2,000 worth of stock and fixtures but had the store back in business three days later. This photograph shows mud, merchandise, and debris from the flood in front of the Capitol Hotel.

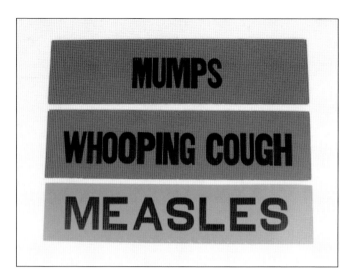

During the flu epidemic of 1918, both of Buffalo's doctors were stricken. Gatchell's training in both pharmacy and veterinary care allowed him to take over patient care, working day and night for extended periods with little sleep. His care was good enough that only six fatalities were reported. These quarantine signs from a local doctor are in the museum's collection and were placed on the front doors of contagious patients' homes.

Jim and Sula Gatchell had three daughters: Thelma, Genevieve, and Clare. Genevieve (left) and Thelma are pictured here as young children. Born in 1901 and earning her degree at the University of Wyoming, Thelma became a teacher in Barnum, Kaycee, and Mayoworth. Genevieve was born in 1904, earned a degree in home economics, and became a homemaker. Clare arrived in 1908.

Clare, the youngest Gatchell daughter, attended pharmacy school at the University of Iowa in Des Moines, where she married classmate David Quale in 1929. They returned to Buffalo to help run the Gatchell Drug Store. David retired in 1957, and Clare retired in 1978. Around 1925, Clare and employee Ferrand Mikesell posed for this photograph inside the store.

From left to right are Jim and Sula Gatchell, Clare Gatchell Quale, Leonard Roudebush, and David Quale in the late 1930s. All except Sula were registered pharmacists. The glass "Prescriptions" sign behind Clare and some of the pharmacy certificates along the back wall are in the museum collection.

Jim and Sula Gatchell's daughters pose with their husbands during Thanksgiving in 1941. From left to right are William and Genevieve Lester, David and Clare Quale, and Clark and Thelma Condit. Thelma died on December 21, 1966, in Buffalo. Genevieve died in Charlotte, North Carolina, on June 8, 1990. Clare followed Genevieve shortly after on November 25, 1990, in Riverton, Wyoming.

Almost all of Jim and Sula Gatchell's grandchildren are in this photograph. The Lesters had daughters Renee and Nova, and the Quales also had two daughters, Marcia and Cynthia. The Condits had three children: Richard ("Dick"), James, and Carolyn. It was Dick who later earned a pharmacy degree and operated the Gatchell Drug Store until its close in 1988.

Native American friends sometimes referred to Gatchell as "Two Belly" for his proportions. He habitually chewed on an unlit cigar, which was seldom removed from his mouth, even when he was talking. Gatchell periodically wore two or three glasses at once, depending on his activity. One pair would be on the tip of his nose, the other on the nose bridge, and the third on his forehead.

Jim Gatchell was awarded the annual Kiwanis Award for Distinguished Community Service in 1950 from the Casper, Wyoming, Chamber of Commerce. He was only the second recipient from Buffalo to receive it. According to the *Casper Star-Tribune*, the choice was one of the most popular ever made by the Casper club, and the 300 guests and chamber of commerce members stood and applauded Gatchell.

Gatchell was bedridden after suffering a stroke in September 1950, shortly after receiving the Kiwanis award. Sula took over his role in the store, working every day with a smile and a friendly greeting. For this, she was recognized by the Business and Professional Women's Club of Buffalo as "the most outstanding businesswoman in our community." In April 1954, after Jim's condition worsened, he was transferred to the Veteran's Hospital in Cheyenne. It was there that he died on June 5, 1954, after four long years of illness, at the age of 81. He was buried at Willow Grove Cemetery in Buffalo. Sula was buried next to him after her death in March 1964 at the age of 87. In this photograph, Jim and Sula Gatchell pose behind a stand of antlers and skulls.

Two

THE ORIGINAL GATCHELL COLLECTION AND THE FOUNDING OF THE MUSEUM

From 1879 to 1888, Jim Gatchell and his family lived near Standing Rock Agency in Dakota Territory. Native Americans were his schoolmates and companions, resulting in Jim appreciating their culture. He learned the Lakota dialect and was adopted into the Sioux tribe at the age of nine and given the name "Good Boy." This photograph shows Chief Young Man Afraid of His Horses at Pine Ridge Agency in South Dakota.

Jim Gatchell's relationships with his Native American friends were revealed in an interview given in 1943. He said, "In the many years that I lived with them, I have never seen an Indian child punished, and I have never heard an Indian—man, woman, or child—take the name of the Lord in vain. The Sioux Indians have a beautiful religion. They believe that the Great Spirit is the embodiment of all that's good. They hold a very high reverence for this Great Spirit that lives in the Sun. That is why the name Sun Dance is given to their dance for the Great Spirit. . . . I saw this dance when I was a child and I am one of the few white men who has seen the genuine sun dance." The photographs above and below show participants at a Sun Dance.

As Gatchell grew older, his continuing desire to learn tribal cultures, beliefs, and languages led him to be adopted into the Northern Cheyenne tribe and given the name "Turpi" or "Turpy" (He Who Speaks For Them). To the Northern Cheyenne, Gatchell was a medicine man who brought good luck. From left to right are Howard Lott, Gatchell, Hard Robe (Cheyenne), and Jean Van Dyke in 1932.

Around 1903, Gatchell found the cylinder of an old cap and ball pistol from the Battle of Little Bighorn. Holding history in his hands, he decided to collect and preserve the history of the region. In this photograph with Gatchell, John Issues, a Cheyenne warrior, is wearing the war bonnet and shield he used during the battle.

Jim Gatchell was trusted by Native Americans and held in high regard because he never made a promise that he did not fulfill. As such, many of the Native American items in the Jim Gatchell Memorial Museum, such as battle regalia, clothing, weapons, and tools, were given to Gatchell as tokens of their esteem and appreciation. Pictured are Mary Weasel Bear, the wife of Weasel Bear, and her grandson Buster.

The Northern Cheyenne would travel hundreds of miles from their reservation to seek Gatchell's medicines or advice. Gatchell sometimes assisted in solving disputes between them and the reservation agents. He would write articles on their behalf explaining their perspectives and viewpoints. Occasionally, when he was younger, Gatchell acted as a translator for an uncle, a US marshal. Here, Gatchell stands with his longtime friend Weasel Bear.

Weasel Bear was a Northern Cheyenne Indian who spent a lot of time around Buffalo visiting with Gatchell. He allowed Gatchell to interview him about Indian War battles and tribal history, and gave Gatchell many artifacts over their years of friendship. As a fellow medicine man, Weasel Bear shared stories and medicinal knowledge with Gatchell. In this photograph, Weasel Bear stands in front of his cabin.

Gatchell also focused on locating frontier-era artifacts. One early artifact added to his collection was this New Model 1859 Carbine Sharps Rifle, found at the 1866 Fetterman Battlefield near Fort Phil Kearny. Gatchell's frontier collection grew to include items from areas and events such as the Bozeman Trail, Wagon Box Fight, Dull Knife Fight, Fort McKinney, and Fort Reno.

Gatchell had a front-row seat to many of the principal actors in many historical events. He met Gen. George Crook, Gen. Ranald Mackenzie, Col. Henry Carrington, Jim Bridger, Frank Grouard (pictured), Portugee Phillips, Curley the Crow, and others through his pharmacy. Not only did he collect tangible artifacts, he also recorded first-person histories from these people.

Jim Gatchell spent over 50 years preserving Johnson County's history, displaying items on his pharmacy's walls. In 1946, he built a large, open room at the back of the store. Visitors from far and wide, including cattlemen, freighters, bullwhackers, trappers, miners, military scouts, soldiers, and settlers came to sit around the potbelly stove and view the collection. Here, Jim and his wife, Sula, are showing the collection to Frank Long.

Jim Gatchell also wrote articles and dedicated historic monuments. Here, he gives a dedication speech during a July 4, 1941, celebration. Gatchell lived in a time when many of the frontier participants were still alive to talk with him, tell their stories, and visit battle sites with him. Gatchell wrote 24 papers on the frontier history of the Powder River country between 1909 and 1950.

Gatchell's "museum" was renowned in that people from throughout the region such as Alex Kerr (left) visited the display, but only one advertisement mentioned the collection. An August 16, 1951, ad in the *Buffalo Bulletin* stated "We cordially invite everyone to see our large collection of Guns and Relics (over 10,000 items). This Collection is worth coming miles to see! No admission fee."

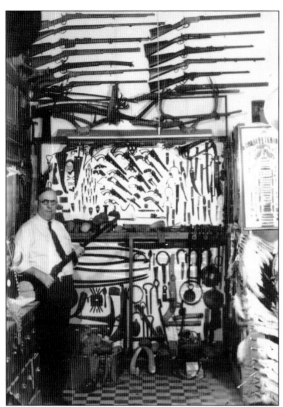

By the time of Gatchell's death in 1954, he had amassed a collection of over 1,200 objects. For a tiny museum in the back of a drug store, he had 7,500 guest signatures from 40 states and Washington, DC, four Canadian provinces, Puerto Rico, and the Canal Zone, according to his summer 1942–summer 1957 guest register. This photograph shows Gatchell posing with his collection.

At the time of Gatchell's death, Johnson County did not have a museum. The Gatchell family expressed interest in donating his collection to the county with the stipulations that a museum bearing Gatchell's name be free to the public and owned and operated by the county, and that the county provide the land for the museum building. Pictured is the Johnson County Courthouse from 1890.

Sam Rosenthall- Arlie Weimer- Dock Rodgers- Pete Jensen- Jack Meldrum- Clarence Gammon- Bob Hancock- Harry Ellis- Geo. Darling- Ray Dixon.   Bud Mead-Monty Hyatt- Bill Long Sr- Geo. Hesse- Clyde Wood- Harold Kaltenbaugh- Geo. Adams- Russell Strother- Ralph Perry- Rev Simms- Ted Wanerus. Harry Gallup- Ray Coulson- Elmer Brock- Glen Kinsley- John Flint- John Hinds- Wilbur Holt- Bert Griggs- Fred Dillinger- Dr.S.E. Krauter.

Members of the Thom and Brock ranching families led the effort to create a county museum. J. Elmer Brock, with the assistance of a supportive committee, planned, designed, and constructed the building. Once completed, it was operated by the county, which oversaw setting up the necessary operational support and legal governance. Pictured are members of the 1942 Buffalo Rotary Club, including Elmer Brock.

A large group of individuals interested in establishing a museum in memory of Jim Gatchell attended an organizational meeting on July 29, 1954, at city hall (left). J. Elmer Brock took the lead in urging that a suitable building be constructed to house the Gatchell collection and other collections. Funds were collected from Johnson County locals and out-of-state donors.

DID YOU KNOW?

THAT JOHNSON COUNTY HAS A VAST, VARIED AND RICH HISTORICAL HERITAGE?

★

The Indians fought hardest and longest to retain this land. It was the main hunting grounds of many Indians and the winter camping headquarters for several tribes. Recent discoveries here are adding tremendously to the knowledge about these early people.

The Portuguese houses, located on Powder River near an old Indian crossing over Powder River where the trails forked to go west to cross the mountains and north into the Big Horn country, served as a trading post and supply base for a vast fur trade. The exact date of the establishment of this post is not known but historians place it between 1807 and 1834.

The Bozeman Trail in this section was more hotly contested by the Indians than any other similar length of any Western Trail.

More forts were located in this county than in any other.

The second greatest number of soldiers killed in any one Indian battle met their death at the Fetterman Massacre.

In a period of 18 months more than 200 men, soldiers and civilians, were killed and over 1400 horses, cows and mules were killed or run off in the Fort Phil Kearney area.

"Portugee" Phillips made his immortal ride for help to save Fort Phil Kearney from destruction.

The Wagon Box Fight, a battle where more Indians were killed than in any other one battle involving whites and Indians, occurred in Johnson County.

Much of the romance and thrilling life in the early "wild west" centered here.

That the Jim Gatchell collection includes more relics from early Indian battles and other Western events than any other single collection.

That the Gatchell family has agreed to turn this valuable collection over to Johnson County IF a suitable building is constructed as a Jim Gatchell Memorial Museum.

That an anonymous donor has agreed to give $50,000.00 if the Johnson County folks will raise $10,000.00 so that this Gatchell collection and many other fine ones can be effectively preserved and not go out of this county.

Now It Is Up To The People of Johnson County

We want to preserve the history of our West and the memories of the people that made it. **LET'S GET BEHIND THE DRIVE TO RAISE THE $10,000.00 AND PUT IT OVER THE TOP!**

If you would care to make a donation at this time, there is a table below the grandstand for this purpose.

This advertisement was printed to promote the establishment of a museum to house the Gatchell collection. It also specified that an anonymous donor had agreed to donate $50,000 if Johnson County citizens would raise $10,000 for the construction of a building so that the collection would not go out of the county. The campaign started in September 1954, and an end date was set for January 31, 1955.

To receive the $50,000 donation, Johnson County had to furnish the grounds and provide funds for the maintenance and service of the museum. The county determined that the best location was near the Johnson County Library (pictured) and the Johnson County Courthouse on Fort Street. The museum building would be able to use the courthouse heating structure, making it easier to maintain.

The $10,000 was raised, but not until April 1955. Strictly a grass-roots effort, most of the donations were in the $5 to $20 range, with only a few $100 or larger donations. Civic organizations held fundraisers of all kinds. By the end of the campaign in August, as seen in this receipt, $11,019.59 was raised from memorial gifts and donations from businesses, individuals, and organizations.

The committee in charge of the planning, design, and construction of the museum included J. Elmer Brock, Robert W. McBride, Helen Meldrum, Wilbur F. Williams (pictured), Thelma Condit, Robert E. Frison, and Peter Meike. Admission fees were discussed, with the decision left to the county commissioners. At the time of the August 1954 meeting, the name Johnson County Jim Gatchell Memorial Museum was formally adopted.

The museum committee advocated creating a permanent local historical society, affiliated with the Wyoming Historical Society, to serve as the primary support group for the museum. This was one of the first tasks it completed, starting the discussion at an August 2, 1954, meeting and ending when the first meeting of the Johnson County Historical Society occurred 18 days later on August 20, 1954. Robert McBride was the first president.

Also attending the first meeting of the Johnson County Historical Society was Cheyenne Indian White Crow from Lame Deer, Montana. He pledged his support and the support of his people to the museum. He stated that Jim Gatchell had been a great friend of his father-in-law Weasel Bear and noted that Indians had helped Gatchell collect his fine exhibit of historical items. This photograph shows White Crow and his family.

The elected museum board included William Kirven, Thelma Condit, Robert Frison, Gene Bennett, Robert McBride, John C. Thom, and Culbertson Brock. Their tasks were to guide the building construction, set up the physical and operational structure, and relocate the collection to its new home. J. Elmer Brock, one of the museum formation leaders, died in 1954. This photograph shows Clark and Thelma Condit as newlyweds.

The proposed location of the museum building next to the Johnson County Library (pictured) was discussed at an August 8, 1955, meeting. Members of the library board insisted that the building not detract from the appearance of the library and that it not be joined to the wall of the library building itself but rather connected by a hallway.

The museum building was a 60-by-30-foot brick and native stone structure, contracted by Charles W. Johnson of Sheridan, Wyoming. Mills Plumbing Shop installed the heating and plumbing. Knepper Electric Supply Store furnished the electrical fixtures. Nielsen's Furniture provided the floor tiles and countertops. Building materials were purchased from Pioneer Lumber Co. and W.F. Smith Lumber Co. The interior equipment and office machines were supplied by the *Buffalo Bulletin*.

The acquisition of display cases and the development of exhibits was the next task of the museum board. They consulted state archivist Lola Homsher, who was very helpful. Richard Condit, Jim Gatchell's grandson, cataloged and transferred the collection into exhibit cases. Alice Anspaugh was hired as a temporary museum custodian/curator.

JOHNSON COUNTY
JIM GATCHELL MEMORIAL MUSEUM
Buffalo, Wyoming

Once the name of the museum was settled on, Gene Bennett expressed the need for museum stationery at an early board meeting. Robert Frison offered to contact local cowboy artist Jesse Winingar for a design. It was completed and sent to the printers in September 1955. This is believed to be the Winingar-designed stationery.

Inside the entrance of the Jim Gatchell Memorial Museum was a small lobby with a desk staffed by a representative of the Buffalo Chamber of Commerce. An office was created for the director of the museum. On the main floor were 12 showcases and five wall cases for the collection, organized by historical eras: prehistoric, Native American, European settlers, Indian Wars, Johnson County Cattle War, and modern history.

Located in the basement were two restrooms and more wall cases. One area of the basement was left bare for hanging heavy items that could not be displayed in cases. Since the beginning, the museum was air-conditioned to maintain a constant temperature and protect the artifacts. Alice Anspaugh, Thelma Condit, Lila Stevenson, and Larry Falxa helped arrange the exhibits for the grand opening.

At the June 5, 1957, board meeting, the museum hours were set as 12:00 p.m. to 8:00 p.m. every day except Sunday, from June through August. Robert Frison was hired as the first director of the museum. He had worked as one of the original Wyoming game wardens until he retired in 1957.

The Johnson County Jim Gatchell Memorial Museum opened to the public on June 11, 1957. The formal dedication occurred on Monday, June 17, at the grade school auditorium with over 500 people in attendance. Gov. Milward Simpson was the main speaker and stated that "Jim saw much of the progress that has come during his own lifetime and I am sorry that he could not have been here today to see this splendid building which has been dedicated to his memory." Richard Condit, Gatchell's grandson, presented the Gatchell collection on behalf of the family. Music was provided by the American Legion Drum and Bugle Corps. This photograph shows the long line that formed as the first guests began their tour of the new museum building. Before evening, more than 400 people had signed the museum register. Many did not stop to sign, wishing to tour the museum. (Courtesy of the *Buffalo Bulletin*.)

Buffalo, Wyo. Under the Big Horn Mts along Clear Creek

The opening-day booklet dedication read, "In arranging the displays we have endeavored to tell something of the history of the Big Horn Mountain region. . . . It was the last great hunting grounds of the Northern Plains Indians. Johnson County, Wyoming, is the heart of this area." Eight years later, Thelma Gatchell Condit wrote,

> The family of Jim Gatchell, in the true spirit of deep western friendship, gave to the people of Johnson County this unusual collection of western and Indian relics, hoping that the beautiful new museum and its historical content will prove an inspiration to all who enter and will instill among them a desire to keep forever alive in their hearts their historical heritage, that they will all come to understand and appreciate the worth of each man who played a part in Johnson County history, for it is only through true knowledge and true understanding of each and every one of them . . . that the memory of Jim Gatchell and the real meaning behind his remarkable collection can . . . live.

This photograph is an overview of the town of Buffalo during its early days.

Three

THE EARLY DAYS OF THE JIM GATCHELL MEMORIAL MUSEUM

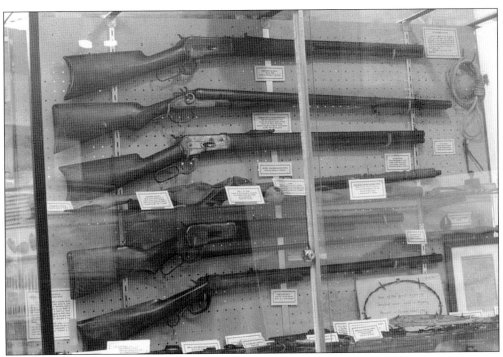

Once the Jim Gatchell Memorial Museum was dedicated, it operated from 12:00 p.m. to 8:00 p.m. Monday through Saturday, from June through August. All employees were essentially part-time, including the first director, Robert Frison, who worked year-round. In the first year, Frison was tasked with making repairs, tagging, and cataloging all new material, and displaying guns that were in the vault.

Natural history was one of the seven subjects covered in the museum. The Wyoming landscape is the result of a series of mountain uplifts followed by erosional leveling. During enormous spans of time, numerous types of animals and plants developed, flourished, and sometimes went extinct. Rocks, fossils (including those of dinosaurs), and animals are just a few of the items exhibited, as seen in the displays behind the shield.

The Jim Gatchell Memorial Museum focuses on the Cheyenne, Crow, Lakota, Shoshone, and Arapaho tribes, as they are the dominant Native American tribes in Wyoming and the High Plains region. All five tribes adopted a nomadic lifestyle, following big game such as bison, deer, elk, and moose. Headdresses, clothing, projectile points, knives, artwork, beadwork, quillwork, and drums make up part of the Native American artifacts displayed in the museum.

The third topic the Jim Gatchell Memorial Museum covered was early settlers such as mountain men, fur trappers, and pioneers who came to Wyoming. The collection includes items from Fort Antonio, an 1834 fur-trading post on the Powder River, and items from pioneers who traveled on the Bozeman and Oregon Trails.

Established to guide pioneers to the gold fields in Montana, the Bozeman Trail was the main thoroughfare through the Powder River country. It also went through the hunting fields of the High Plains Indians. Numerous skirmishes along the trail led to the establishment of forts such as Reno, Phil Kearny, and C.F. Smith. The museum contains many artifacts from the Indian Wars, as seen in this photograph.

The Johnson County Cattle War was a conflict between "cattle barons" of the Wyoming Stock Growers Association and individual ranchers and homesteaders. The invasion in April 1892 and the three-day siege at the TA Ranch were the watershed events of the war. As a result of this conflict and other factors, the cattle industry never fully returned to the economic stature it achieved during the territorial years. This photograph shows cattle war items.

The last subject the museum covered was modern history. Items from businesses on Main Street, including the Buffalo Drug Store and Jim Gatchell's personal collection, were included. Photographs of community organizations and the Buffalo Diamond Jubilee (1884–1959) represent a small portion of this category in the museum collection.

Over the years, saddles and bridles have been donated to the museum, including examples from Native American tribes and local Johnson County citizens, as well as saddle remnants found along emigrant trails and creeks. The styles include ladies' side saddles and US military McClellan saddles. There are also saddle items from local Buffalo saddle maker Percy "P.A." Wilkerson. This photograph showcases some of the saddles in the collection.

The museum had a stable, consistent board of trustees from 1957 to 1987. John C. Thom held the chairman position from 1957 to 1962 before becoming a board member at large until 1977. William Kirven was elected chairman in 1962 and served until 1988, when Helen Meldrum assumed the position. Here, she is posing in historical dress for the Buffalo Diamond Jubilee.

Culbertson Brock served as the vice chairman of the board of trustees from 1957 to 1972. James Dillinger then served as vice chair from 1973 to 1987. From the beginning of the Jim Gatchell Memorial Museum, Robert McBride served as treasurer for 30 years until 1988. This is Dillinger's 1941 senior photo from the Johnson County High School yearbook.

Gatchell family descendants continued to stay active in the Jim Gatchell Memorial Museum. Thelma Gatchell Condit served as secretary for the board of trustees from 1957 to 1968. Then her son, Jim Gatchell's grandson Richard Condit, served in that capacity until 1988, when Dolly Fraley was elected to the position. Pictured is a gathering of Gatchell and Sackett family members.

During the museum governing board's two meetings held in 1958, it was reported that the Johnson County commissioners accepted their $4,005.25 budget for the coming year. They also discussed whether to create a gift shop to sell books. The last item discussed was whether to expand the museum hours to Sundays. The commissioners have operated out of the Johnson County Courthouse (pictured) since 1884.

The main issue discussed in the 1959 meetings was water collecting in the museum basement. John C. Thom thought Johnson County would cover the repairs. He also informed the board that Pioneer Lumber Co. across the street had the same issue, which was remedied by installing a sump pump. He was authorized to investigate and collect bids for the work. Pictured is a Christmas card from Pioneer Lumber Co.

The lone 1960 board meeting was on August 23, when the board met to discuss executive officer positions. The issue on the table was that repairs in 1959 did not solve the water problem in the museum's basement. The board determined that Bill Kirven and John C. Thom would bring the matter to the Johnson County commissioners. Pictured are exhibits in the museum basement.

The water saga continued in 1961, according to meeting minutes from June 27. The sump pump had not been installed, as the board was trying to avoid expenses. Also discussed was an offered gun collection that the board decided not to purchase as it did not want to establish a precedent of buying items for the museum. Pictured are more exhibits from the museum basement.

At the July 13, 1962, meeting, the board discussed two items. First, the board decided to fund three wooden, arrowhead-shaped street signs to advertise the museum, to be installed in 1963. Two would be placed east of town and one west. Second, the donation of a large collection that necessitated the purchase of an additional case to display the items. One of the arrowhead signs is pictured here.

In the 1963 meeting minutes, the museum's "multiplex" for the display of historical photographs was mentioned for the first time. As seen in this photograph, it is still being used today in the introductory gallery. The water in the basement was finally dealt with, as the museum budgeted for sump pump installation.

In his 1964 obituary, it was revealed that the anonymous donor of $50,000 for the establishment of the museum was William B. Thom. Thom grew up in Buffalo, attended college at the University of Michigan, and became president of the Warner Chemical Company, which merged with FMC Corp. In addition to the museum donation, he, his wife, and the rest of the Thom siblings created the well-known Thom Scholarship to send deserving men and women to college. It has been established since 1944 and is still awarded to Buffalo High School seniors. Two years after Thom died, the Jim Gatchell Memorial Museum's first director, Robert Frison, resigned. Stuart Frazier became the second director, serving until 1970. Later, George Barkley was hired as director, and held the position until 1983, when Lee Campbell took over until 1990. While acting as directors, the official titles of these men were listed as curators in the meeting minutes.

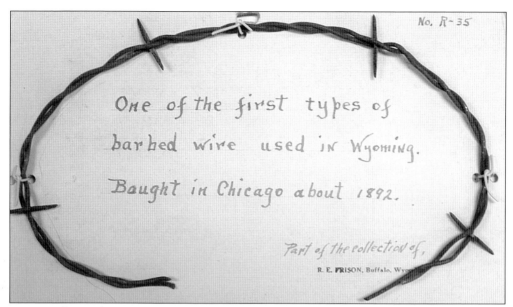

In 1966, when Robert Frison resigned, William Kirven approached Frison to ask about bestowing his collection to the museum. Frison's collection included fossil specimens of dinosaurs, ammonites, and insects; Native American stone weapons and tools; a World War I first aid kit; arrowhead points; and other miscellaneous objects such as this barbed wire. While the collection was on display in the museum, it was not officially gifted until 1987.

For much of the first 30 years of the Jim Gatchell Memorial Museum, it was only open seasonally, in spring and summer, and closed during the winter months. Special tours were available during the off-season if arrangements were made. The board of directors met yearly between April and May, with occasional winter meetings to discuss maintenance issues. This photograph shows visitors enjoying the upstairs displays.

In 1988, the Johnson County Library erected a new building. The board of directors, now meeting monthly, approached the county commissioners about acquiring the 1909 Carnegie Library for expansion purposes. The building was allocated to the museum, which remodeled the interior and used it as a museum annex. The first floor became a store, with antique display cases from the Purcell Jewelry Store (pictured) purchased for merchandise.

The museum store merchandise included books, Native American items, souvenirs, postcards, maps, artwork, home furnishings, and more. The original desk from the Johnson County Library was used as the admission and store counter, as seen here. Museum hours for the season were extended into October and then into November.

Four

Expansion of the Jim Gatchell Memorial Museum

The Jim Gatchell Memorial Museum hired director Gary Anderson in 1990. He was the first director to have a degree in anthropology, extensive business knowledge, experience working in museums, and a lifelong avocation for regional history. He was instrumental in initiating a formal collections conservation program, updating exhibits, and developing a staff of employees and volunteers. Supporting Anderson was an administrative assistant and a collections manager.

The board of directors focused on developing a "hands-on" children's corner in early 1990 and unveiled it in May. They reported it was a success, with lots of locals coming in. Tourists, particularly parents, were especially appreciative. A permanent children's corner was installed in the basement of the Carnegie building in 1996, as seen here.

Part of the Gatchell descendants' stipulations was that the museum charge no admission, but by the early 1990s, Wyoming's oil boom had collapsed. With limited county funds to operate, the board determined it was legal to charge admission. For the 1992 season, admission of $2 for adults was charged. The museum also adopted a marketing slogan of "Jim Gatchell Museum of the West," as displayed on this sign.

To address the declining tax base, in late 1991, concerned Johnson County citizens incorporated the Gatchell Museum Association Inc. (GMA) to provide financial support to the museum and establish an endowment fund. The GMA became a dedicated "friends" organization, helping with marketing, membership, and fundraising. It also developed a newsletter called the *Sentry*. The museum logo, seen on this sign, was updated and adopted by the GMA.

In December 1992, the board decided that a carriage house needed to be built to enclose the museum's historic wagons for conservation purposes instead of being displayed outside. The project was funded through campaigns such as selling bricks for a Memory Lane and wood panels for brands. Involved in the development were family members of Robert "Bob" Gibbs and William "Bill" Norton, who helped restore the wagons over the years.

As the carriage house addition project progressed, in 1997, the board sought further funding from the Johnson County commissioners for the installation of an elevator, hallway, and storage space. Funds were allocated to the museum by the commissioners in early 1998. Construction on the addition would occur when the carriage house project began. Pictured is the carriage house with the museum addition plan.

Construction began on the carriage house and addition in the summer of 1998 under the direction of general contractor and longtime museum volunteer Franklin Edward "Ed" Crain. The project progressed steadily except for a broken foot suffered by worker Scott Madsen and the abandonment of plans for storage space in the addition. The dedication and open house for the projects was on June 6, 1999.

Carriage house construction continued after the dedication. The wagons were not relocated until interior construction was completed. Once finished in November 2000, the wagons were moved to their permanent home. To celebrate, on June 27, 2001, the museum held a wagon train parade down Main Street as part of Living History Day festivities.

In 1994, in efforts to modernize, the Jim Gatchell Memorial Museum sought and was awarded a Museum Assessment Program (MAP1) grant by the American Alliance of Museums. This grant assessed and suggested improvements to administration, exhibits, programs, facilities, planning, collections, governance, membership, and community support. The museum received adequate, good, and excellent evaluations in all but collections. Pictured is a board committee meeting.

Based on the MAP1 report, the museum developed a five-year strategic plan. The objectives were to become nationally accredited by AAM and to hire a professional museum conservator. National accreditation is tangible evidence that the highest professional standards in a museum's programs, operations, and activities have been met and maintained. AAM represents all museums, staff, and volunteers and assists in the overall professional development of museums.

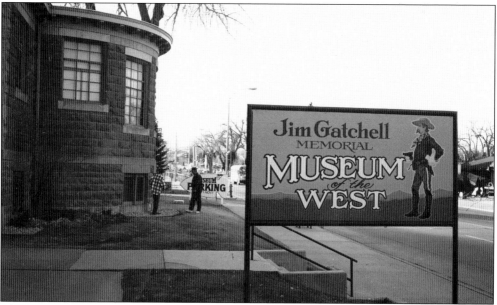

The museum began working on accreditation by updating and developing policies such as governance, ethics, collections management, membership, and security to better reflect the standards of AAM. Once the policies were adopted, director Gary Anderson began the accreditation process with AAM in December 1998. The application was submitted in May 1999. The museum rebranded itself again at this time as the Jim Gatchell Memorial Museum of the West.

The accreditation process continued, with revisions requested from AAM. The museum was given a deadline of May 1, 2000, for resubmission. The resubmitted application was approved and sent to the review committee in November, which accepted it. The next step, a site visit, occurred in June 2000. Staff, board members, and volunteers participated. This photograph shows one of the volunteers undertaking collections work.

While waiting for the scheduled site visit, the museum adopted a policy regarding the Native American Graves Protection and Repatriation Act. This policy related to the handling of culturally sensitive items in the collection, which consisted of 2,600 archaeological artifacts and 150 ethnographic artifacts. This policy completed the museum's compliance with accreditation.

After the site visit, the board determined that it needed a new five-year plan. Board members met at the Pines Lodge (now YMCA of the Bighorns Camp Roberts) on September 15, 2000. They decided the next priorities included marketing, a Carnegie wing exterior addition, fundraising, internships, and strengthening of the staff. This photograph shows some of the museum marketing activity during Living History Days.

As part of its new five-year plan, the board decided to raise the admission rate. Beginning in the summer of 2001, adults were charged $4, families $7, senior citizens $3, and ages six to sixteen $2. Children five and under were admitted free. Funds from admissions went toward expanding the museum store, hiring a full-time curator, and increasing museum advertising. Volunteers and visitors are seen in this photograph.

The AAM site visit results asked for changes to be made before moving forward. In January 2001, the board had to decide whether to make the changes requested or drop accreditation. They decided to continue, and the final paperwork was submitted on January 8, 2002, one year after the revision was requested. The Jim Gatchell Memorial Museum finally was awarded accreditation in 2002. Pictured is a board meeting from that time.

The museum staff expanded to include a part-time collections technician in October 2000. The position was offered to Robert Wilson. Later, museum staff expanded again with the hiring of Jean Dean as a new assistant to the museum director in January 2001. When registrar Sunny Taylor (pictured) resigned in March 2001, the new part-time registrar was Linda Newell, who served until July 2003.

Gary Anderson notified the museum board in August 2001 that he wished to retire in 2003. The board began the search for a new director in early 2002. After discussion about the applicants, an offer was extended to John Gavin (pictured) from Cheyenne Frontier Days Old West Museum in Cheyenne. He accepted and became the director on January 6, 2003.

In 2002, Gatchell descendants held a family reunion in Buffalo to celebrate the 130th anniversary of Jim Gatchell's birth. Hats from Ursula Gatchell Sackett were worn by many of the women. Here, some of the family members pose on the front steps of the museum.

Jean Dean left the museum in August 2003, and the search for a new assistant director began. The new assistant director would focus predominantly on museum education and increasing programming. Robert Edwards (pictured) was hired as the new educator in July 2004. Sylvia Jackman was hired as the new part-time registrar in October 2003. She became full-time and the sole registrar in September 2005.

Exhibits planned at the museum during the 1990s and early 2000s included Basque history, the Bozeman Trail, Portuguese houses, Dull Knife Battle, Bernard Thomas studio, and Bomber Mountain. Exhibit upgrade training was undertaken by museum volunteer William "Bill" Payne (standing) in 1999 when he attended a seminar on how to upgrade exhibits for small museums.

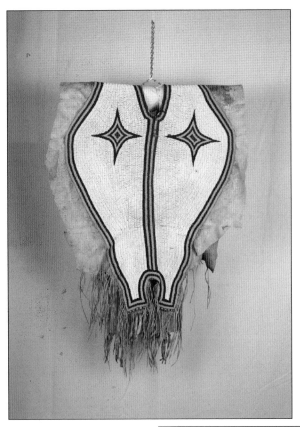

In September 1998, the museum became the repository for 11 Northern Cheyenne artifacts confiscated by Gen. Anson Mills from the Battle of Slim Buttes on September 9–10, 1876, in South Dakota. They were held by his family until personal repatriation occurred. Pictured is a poncho with a beautiful and clear representation of the original morning star design, identified by Gilbert Whitedirt and Nancy Sandcrane.

Beginning in 2004, museum staff and volunteers began attending conferences, seminars, and workshops to develop skills in collections management, exhibits, and interpretation. A full inventory of the museum's artifacts was conducted at the same time. For the next five years, the concentration was on developing a thematic and chronological framework for the museum galleries. Here, two volunteers conduct collections work in the gallery.

In November 2004, the museum started the Jim Gatchell Memorial Museum Press to publish works on local and regional history. The first book was *South Pass 76ers: A Wyoming Gold Rush* by Gil Bollinger. The press expanded to include eight Big Horn Tales booklets and ten books. Here, Bollinger (right) is promoting his *Jim Gatchell, The Man and The Museum* book.

Since the late 1980s, the museum had been operating out of two structures: the original building and the old Carnegie Library (pictured). Discussion began in early 2005 about creating a link between the two and having the museum become fully American Disabilities Act compliant. By July, the board officially moved forward with a tentative budget of $250,000 for the link.

Construction began on the link addition on July 20, 2006, with a projected completion date of November 30. Can-Do Construction from Casper, Wyoming, oversaw construction, and Plan One Architects from Cody, Wyoming, managed the project. It created an additional storage room entered from the collections lab, an elevator, stairs, and a tool shop, and enclosed an existing exterior stairwell. It was finished in February 2007 after a few months of delay. This photograph shows the link and stairwell being built between the two buildings. The exterior of the Carnegie building is in the background. The publications committee, consisting of members from the Gatchell Museum Association Inc., and the Jim Gatchell Memorial Museum Press, decided to reformat the quarterly newsletter the *Sentry* to a magazine-style publication in June 2006. The first issue to receive the new treatment was January 2007, appropriately dedicated to celebrating 50 years of the Jim Gatchell Memorial Museum.

Five

THE MODERN JIM GATCHELL MEMORIAL MUSEUM

The new thematic and chronological framework of the Jim Gatchell Memorial Museum's galleries began with the Natural West and Native West galleries in late 2008. A diorama featuring a pronghorn and other animals was created in the new Natural West gallery, seen here. Lynn Stewart, who created the dioramas at the Northeast Wyoming Regional Airport in Gillette, Wyoming, was the taxidermist.

The museum expanded its historical wagon collection when Emerson Scott Sr. donated a six-mule US Army wagon (pictured), a four-mule US Army wagon, and a doctor's buggy in September 2008. These were originally featured at Bozeman Trail Steakhouse in Buffalo. Additionally, Scott donated a log-hauling sled. These are all on display in the carriage house.

Before the Bozeman Trail gallery exhibits fabrication in 2010, two projects took place. The storage room that was removed from the 1998 carriage house plans was finally constructed. This space consolidated archival material such as documents, letters, newspapers, and books in one location. Later, the museum's saddle collection and larger artifact boxes were also included. The second project was the installation of the interactive Bozeman Trail map (pictured).

John Gavin began advertising for a new museum educator in November 2008 as Robert Edwards stated his intent to retire in April 2009. The search was closed on May 12. Jennifer Romanoski (pictured) was hired and started the position in August 2009. As of the publication of this book, she is still the museum educator.

The museum worked with the Wyoming Department of Transportation beginning in 2008 on the beautification of the museum lawn and exterior. In addition to D. Michael Thomas's Nate Champion statue (see page 127), the project included rock work extending from the statue base along the sidewalk to the corner of Fort and Main Streets. Franklin Edward "Ed" Crain installed the rock work, as seen here.

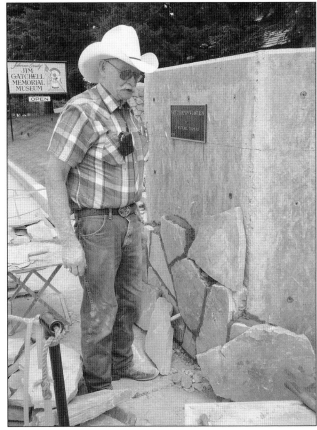

Projects completed in 2010 included the Bozeman Trail gallery and the interactive Gatchell Drug Store exhibit, revamping museum policies, and updating the museum's mission statement. The Bozeman Trail gallery (pictured) highlighted the emigrant trail, the Indian Wars of the 1860s, Buffalo Soldiers, and forts established along the trail. At the end of the year, the board participated in a retreat to develop a new five-year plan.

Through anonymous donations and a Rocky Mountain Power grant, the museum was able to update the galleries to LED lighting, which was recommended by AAM as optimum for the care and preservation of the artifacts on display. Pictured is registrar Sylvia (Jackman) Bruner processing artifacts in a museum gallery.

During 2011, museum staff and volunteers were dedicated to updating and remodeling the Johnson County Cattle War and Basque galleries. The previously designed "Almost Like Home . . . The Basque Along The Big Horns" exhibit was relocated from the carriage house, as seen here, and moved to a permanent gallery to fit the chronological timeline the museum had developed.

Also in 2011, the museum conducted a much-needed project on Vance Lucas's projectile points collection, working with high school interns. The collection included over 7,500 projectile points and a hand-written ledger from Lucas detailing where and when the points were found and by whom. Most were from around Johnson County. The inside cover of the handwritten ledger is pictured here.

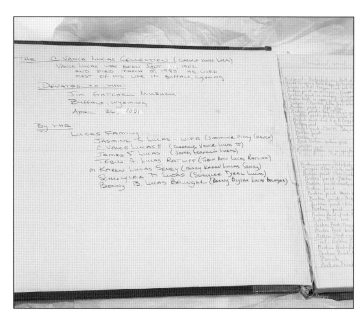

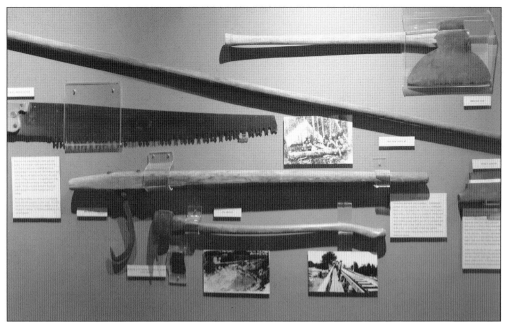

In 2012, the museum exhibits committee began work on an updated Bomber Mountain exhibit and smaller exhibits within the Local Buffalo History gallery. These smaller exhibits have highlighted the arson fire on Main Street in 1988, the Clear Creek Flood of 1912, the time a Boeing 737 mistakenly landed at the Buffalo Airport in 1979, tie hacking in the Bighorn National Forest (pictured), and the Black and Yellow Trail.

The last museum gallery to be remodeled was the Changing Exhibits gallery. Designed to host temporary exhibits for two or three years, the first installation to premiere was a painting retrospective on local artist Mel Gerhold in 2012. Later exhibits included military uniforms, Cloud Peak Wilderness photographs celebrating the 50th anniversary of the Wyoming Wilderness Act (pictured), the Wyoming state flag anniversary, early Buffalo businesses, and more.

When the gallery remodels were nearing completion, the museum board and staff turned to updating and remodeling the museum store beginning in 2012. The store was renovated with new furnishings, lighting, and arrangements to create a more productive space. As part of this new remodel, Barbara Hartley was hired as the store manager in March 2012. This photograph shows the installation of walls to create two offices.

In April 2012, a retail consultant determined that the store had too large a footprint and too much inventory. Using grant money and donations, construction on the store remodel (updating the carpeting, installing office walls, and purchasing new fixtures) commenced in the fall of 2013. The remodeled store was unveiled in May 2014. Pictured is the new children's area.

Since 1957, the Jim Gatchell Memorial Museum had operated on a summer season schedule, with winter closures from January through April. After the extensive exhibit remodeling, the museum began opening year-round in the fall of 2012. With the increase of artifacts in storage to fit the new exhibit design, the museum advertised for a full-time collections assistant in early 2013. Jessica Knight was hired in May 2013.

In March 2015, an anonymous donation was used to purchase eight new Dorfman museum mannequins, which allowed clothing and uniforms to be displayed more safely and realistically than previous mannequins could. They were used in the Uniform Stories: Johnson County Dressed for Service exhibit, which highlighted eight uniforms from Johnson County veterans in the collection.

The year 2016 was a time of upheaval and change at the museum. Due to decreasing county funds, the position of collections assistant was eliminated, and Jessica Knight left in May. Also because of funding shortages, director John Gavin asked for an advance from the Johnson County commissioners, causing great concern in the community. He later resigned and left the museum in May. Registrar Sylvia Bruner (pictured) became the new director.

Funding became a major concern of the staff and museum board after the departure of John Gavin. It was not known if the museum would continue with the deficit of operating funds. Staff and volunteers stepped up to operate the store and museum on summer weekends instead of hiring summer staff. New bookkeeping procedures were developed to provide more transparency. Pictured is museum volunteer Nancy Pedro in 2016.

AAM re-accreditation began in March 2016, with a site visit in July. After the site visit, a new strategic plan was developed and the governing structure between Johnson County and the museum was clarified. A memorandum of understanding was adopted stating the museum was a county ancillary. With these updates, re-accreditation was awarded in March 2018, with staff seen posing with the certificate.

The museum began a yearly exhibit remodel in 2017. Each year since, one gallery was targeted, with artifacts rotated out and labels updated to reflect new research and artifacts. The Native West gallery (pictured) and carriage house were updated in 2018, the Changing Exhibits gallery in 2019 and 2021, and the History of Buffalo gallery in 2019 and 2020.

Addressing continued declining county revenue, the museum board decided in March 2017 to raise admission prices. Adults were charged $7, seniors $5, and tour rates $5. Children were broken down into three categories: five and under were free, ages six through eleven were $3, and twelve through eighteen were $5. These increases helped alleviate the 36 percent budget decrease in 2017–2018 and the further 15 percent decrease in 2018–2019.

The museum adopted its current calendar in 2017. Summer hours (Memorial Day through Labor Day) are Monday through Saturday 9:00 a.m.–5:00 p.m. and Sundays 12:00 p.m.–5:00 p.m. Winter hours, from September through May, are 9:00 a.m.–4:00 p.m. Monday through Friday. The museum is closed to the public in February for collections, maintenance, and exhibit work. Pictured are artifacts acquired in 2020.

Store manager Barbara Hartley left the museum in December 2017. Due to a hiring freeze by the county commissioners, the museum staff and board did not know if they would be able to refill the position. The museum rallied and solicited community letters of support advocating for the replacement of the third member of the permanent full-time museum staff. Museum assistant Kelsey McDonnell (pictured) was hired in April 2018.

The museum recognized the need to create more storage space for artifacts in the mid-2000s. A restricted fund made up of donations and memorials was started for the purchase of condensed shelving units. Over 15 years, the fund steadily grew, and with grant money from the Tucker Foundation, the new units were installed in November 2017.

Together with the Gatchell Museum Association, the museum rebuilt its website and underwent a complete rebranding in early 2018. Both the museum and the GMA unveiled new logos later that year. Continued rebranding efforts include revamped covers of the *Sentry* starting in 2019, new interior and exterior museum signage, and covers of the historic walking and driving tour brochures in 2022.

The aging structure of the Carnegie building made a new roof necessary in 2017. Discussion began in February 2018. County funds needed to be procured, and the Wyoming State Historic Preservation Office needed to be consulted, as the building has been listed in the National Register of Historic Places since 1978. Funds and permission were secured and the new roof was installed in June 2020, as seen here.

COVID-19 caused the museum to shut down from March to May 2020, and staff worked remotely. By direction of the Johnson County commissioners, the museum reopened on May 1 with several COVID-related changes in place. All interactive portions of exhibits were temporarily closed, all touch surfaces were disinfected frequently, a sneeze guard was installed at the front desk, and limitations were put in place regarding the number of people in the museum at one time. Staff furthermore developed COVID-themed products to sell in the museum store. One was a COVID-themed t-shirt in collaboration with Surf Wyoming. The back read, "DO NOT APPROACH BUFFALO, We recommend more than 6 feet social distancing in Wyoming." Themed masks were created as well, featuring the Wyoming state flag, Crazy Woman Canyon, and even Christmas-themed masks during the holidays. This photograph shows the COVID-themed merchandise sold in 2020 and 2021.

The staff and board were grateful that COVID-19 did not greatly affect the operation of the museum. Much of the in-person summer programming was canceled except for the Echoes of the Past cemetery tours. As part of the nationwide social media "A World of Hearts" campaign, staff placed hearts in the windows along Fort Street to inspire hope and to cheer up the Buffalo community.

The museum began discussions regarding highway signs with the Wyoming Department of Transportation (WYDOT) as early as the late 1990s. WYDOT determined that the museum qualified for the highway signs at no cost. The three highway signs and three off-ramp signs on Interstates 90 West, 25 North, and 90 East were installed in July 2020.

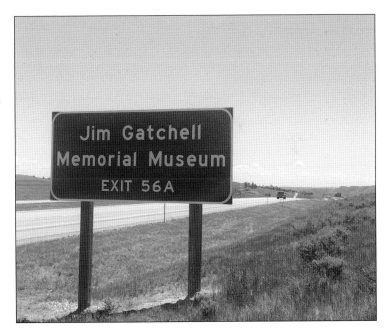

Maintenance proceeded both inside and outside the museum in the mid-2010s. Metal railings (above) and a new ramp for the Jenkins Homestead cabin (see page 125) were installed in 2018. New HVAC systems replaced the aging, non-efficient furnaces that almost caused a fire in 2019. The elevator and lift were serviced in 2021 and 2022. Most recently, the trim, windows, doors, and soffits of the Carnegie building were painted in 2021 by KARS Kustom Painting (left). The staff and museum board became aware that the north end of the homestead cabin was sinking and causing cracks to appear in the structure. In 2022, stabilization of the foundation occurred. Currently, the museum is focused on the repointing and resealing of the Carnegie Library building to stabilize the sandstone exterior.

Six

CONTINUING JIM GATCHELL'S LEGACY THROUGH EVENTS AND PROGRAMS

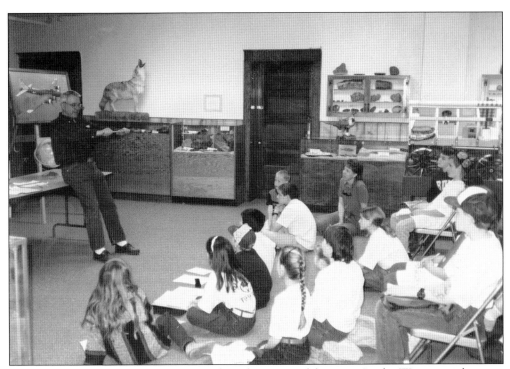

Since the early days of the museum, students have visited for tours. In the Wyoming education curriculum, local and regional history is covered during fourth grade. In 1998, the museum saw a marked increase, with students visiting from the communities of Buffalo, Ranchester, Kaycee, Sheridan, and Casper. Today, the museum still plays host to springtime school tours. In this photograph, Gil Bollinger educates students in the museum basement.

One of the first educational programs developed at the museum outside of school tours was Jim Gatchell's Living History Day in 1990. It was originally established as a three-to-four-day program with free exhibits, demonstrations, a parade, lectures, and re-enactments. Today, Living History Day continues as a day-long event of demonstrations and hands-on activities. In this photograph, volunteer Brucie Connell is spinning wool during a Living History Day event.

The second educational program was a two-day program for all third-grade students called Early Days in Buffalo. It introduced students to the ranching and agricultural history of Buffalo through the museum's collections and resources. The museum collaborated with Johnson County School District No. 1 and implemented the program in 1995. The museum no longer offers this program. Pictured is an early photograph of Buffalo's Main Street.

In 1996, History and Coffee was established. It was a chance for Johnson County citizens to gather at the museum during winter months to recall and share family and community history like Basque history, as pictured here with Basque children Grace and Mitchell Esponda. The museum provided videotapes, books, informal lectures, and the occasional collection item to promote dialogue among the participants. This program was discontinued in late 2013.

The first annual history conference occurred in 1997 with the theme Cattlemen vs. Sheepmen—5 Decades of Violence in the West. For three days, attendees enjoyed presentations, dinner, and a tour of the Tensleep, Wyoming, Spring Creek historic battle site. Later topics for one-day conferences included frontier medicine, centennial ranches, the musical heritage of Wyoming, and more. This photograph shows a history conference at the Johnson County Fairgrounds.

In the late 1990s, the museum offered a series of tours to historic areas as fundraising and educational events. The historic TA Ranch, the site of the three-day siege during the Johnson County Cattle War, was visited. Other historic area tours included the Hole-in-the-Wall country where Butch Cassidy and the Sundance Kid operated (pictured), Rosebud battlefield, Bozeman Trail forts, and Dull Knife Battlefield.

One of museum educator Robert Edwards's first programs was a seminar series called Powder River Round Table. Unlike History and Coffee, this series offered a more formal setting and was conducted in the evening in partnership with the Occidental Hotel. Later, he taught a Johnson County/Wyoming history class developed with Sheridan College in Sheridan, Wyoming. Pictured is an early photograph of the Occidental Saloon.

The Echoes of the Past cemetery tours started in 2005. These nighttime tours in Willow Grove Cemetery feature first-person oral histories by volunteers. The first cast included William "Red" Angus, John Tisdale, Jim Gatchell, Nate Champion, "Mourning Mother," and Andrew "Arapaho" Brown. Tickets cost $10, and there were four performances: one in July, two in August, and one in September. Pictured are costumed volunteers from the cemetery tours.

The cemetery tours continue to be one of the museum's most popular programs. Tours have expanded to eight performances over two weeks in August, and tickets cost $25. Historical characters are still portrayed, as well as people with a Buffalo connection. Here, Lynn Young as August Hettinger enthralls attendees.

One of the first educational programs developed by museum educator Jennifer Romanoski was a series of walking tours and brochures that covered the Buffalo Railway (pictured), streets and homes, historic Main Street, Johnson County National Register of Historic Places sites, and natural history. Additionally, she worked with fourth-grade teachers to develop a children's activity book. These tours and brochures have been printed since 2010 and were rebranded in 2022.

The museum expanded its school programs in 2010 to include a second-grade dinosaur program and a first-grade rock program. After first partnering with Michael Dawson of the T-Rex Natural History Museum in Ranchester, Wyoming, for the dinosaur program (pictured), later partnerships included local paleontologists and archaeologists. The rock program was the first partnership the museum developed with the Bureau of Land Management.

School programs have expanded to include first-grade programs Light and Sound, Sage Grouse, and Native American history, second-grade program Neighborhoods and Public Art (pictured), third-grade programs Main Street Businesses: Resources, Needs, and Wants and Streets and Community, and more. Collaborations with community organizations such as the US Forest Service, the Bureau of Land Management, and Wyoming State Forestry occur as the need for new programs grows.

Beginning in November 2010, Fun at the Museum was offered on federal holidays when school was not in session. For three hours, participants enjoyed activities and crafts related to a specific theme such as recycled crafts, veterans' history, bugs and insects, and Basque history. This program was discontinued in 2016 when school calendars changed. In this photograph, attendees make volcanoes as part of a Natural Phenomenon theme.

The museum began connecting with homeschoolers and offered up to seven programs a year beginning in September 2012. As attendance grew, programs reflected a multi-age approach to teaching and themes better related to the museum's collection and mission, with an emphasis on STEM (science, technology, engineering, math) and STEAM (science, technology, engineering, art, math). It was discontinued during COVID-19 in 2021. Here, homeschoolers participate in a constellations and space-themed program.

Developing partnerships with the local Boys & Girls Club and the Johnson County YMCA, the museum offered once-a-week summer camp programs in 2016. Participants learned about various topics such as architecture on Main Street, conducted science experiments, toured Willow Grove Cemetery, spelunked through a cave obstacle course, and were introduced to Project Learning Tree activities, seen here. These camps were offered until 2019.

With donations and proceeds from Frackelton's Restaurant/Sheridan Media's Dining for a Cause fundraiser, the museum was able to sponsor STEM-based wildfire programs in partnership with the US Forest Service, the Bureau of Land Management, and Wyoming State Forestry in 2017. Topics covered included wildfire management, fire science and technology, and a site visit to the 2014 West Range forest fire (pictured).

The museum celebrated the 125th anniversary of the Johnson County Cattle War with a symposium on September 15–16, 2017. Included was an author's panel, Grandpa's Stories, which invited community members from both sides of the war to share family stories passed down about the war, and a reenactment of the three-day siege at the TA Ranch (pictured). The reenactment was filmed for a future documentary.

Continuing efforts to highlight sensitive topics such as race, intolerance, and injustice, the museum hosted Japanese American Sam Mihara in March 2018. Mihara (pictured) visited with students and community members about his experiences as a youth at Heart Mountain Internment Camp during World War II. Later, in September, John Griffin described his experiences as one of the "Black 14" football players in 1969 at the University of Wyoming.

The museum continued these programming efforts with Northern Arapaho Yufna Soldier Wolf (pictured) presenting about the Carlisle Indian School and her efforts to repatriate her tribe's three deceased children back to the Wind River Reservation in Wyoming. In 2020, the museum partnered with the Johnson County Historical Society to present a program on the 75th anniversary of the liberation of World War II concentration camp Auschwitz.

The museum began offering more Native American programs, presented by Native Americans, in 2019. It hosted Northern Cheyenne ledger artist Alaina Buffalo Spirit to present art workshops in the school and community in January (pictured). Later, three scholars—Northern Arapaho Yufna Soldier Wolf, Eastern Shoshone John Washakie, and Minniconjou Lakota/Cheyenne Donovin Sprague—were the presenters at the Native American Cultures history conference.

Art Museum Mondays began in 2019. Occurring every Monday in June and July, these programs were geared toward children between the ages of six and eleven who enjoyed art activities with a coordinating book component. Activities included chalk art, mural painting, clay modeling, still lifes of donkeys (pictured), felting, and painting. First funded by donations, funds from the Hazel Patterson Memorial Grant were later used to expand and continue this program.

Wine About History began in the summer of 2019 and was designed as a free outdoor lecture series with attendees bringing their own chairs and beverage of choice, as seen in this photograph. Themes included the history of sheep wagons, big-game migration, Native American history of the Bozeman Trail, Johnson County journalism, and others. It was later rebranded Sip N' History and relocated to the carriage house.

COVID-19 caused the museum to shut down for two months in 2020. During that time, the museum provided 150 small art kits to local children. It also developed Grow with the Gatchell, a series of history-themed YouTube videos, with supplementary links and activities on the museum's website. In one, the museum educator's rubber duck collection was used to portray the Johnson County Cattle War (pictured).

When the 2020–2021 school year started, an anonymous donation allowed for the installation of Wi-Fi throughout the museum for virtual programming. Previously, the museum's Wi-Fi was only accessible in the Carnegie building of the museum complex. For much of the school year, previously developed programs such as Rocks, Neighborhoods, Dinosaurs, and others were adapted and tailored to be presented virtually. The 2021 history conference celebrating centennial ranches in Johnson County was presented virtually as well after being canceled in 2020. Pictured are the virtual Neighborhoods program (above) and the virtual Dinosaurs program (below) with Randolph Moses, the principal paleontologist for Absaroka Energy and Environmental Solutions.

Over the years, the programs at the Jim Gatchell Memorial Museum have earned state and regional educational awards. In 2018, museum educator Jennifer Romanoski received the Wyoming State Historical Society's Henryetta Berry Memorial Award, bestowed to an individual or organization in recognition of their years of encouraging young people to learn, share, and love Wyoming's history. Only one award is presented a year, and it does not need to be awarded each year. Museum assistant Kelsey McDonnell (pictured) received the 2021 EDCOM Award for Programming Excellence for her Art Museum Mondays program. This award is voted on by educators across the 10 states that make up the Mountain Plains Museum Association and recognizes exemplary creativity and innovation in museum educational programming. The award is given to one recipient from small museums (less than $250,000 annual budget), mid-sized museums ($250,001–500,000), and large-sized museums ($500,001 and up).

Seven

TREASURES FROM THE JIM GATCHELL MEMORIAL MUSEUM COLLECTION

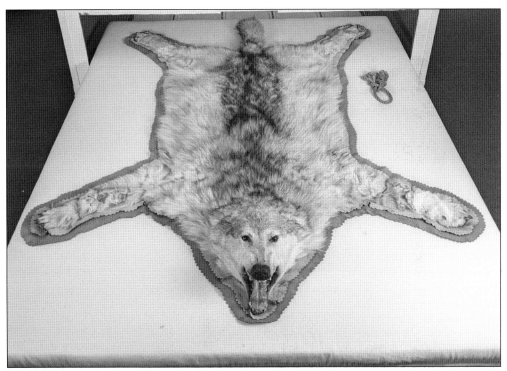

Johnson County rancher J. Elmer Brock shot this wolf in 1909 when it was attacking his livestock. He donated the pelt to the museum in the 1970s. Displayed for many years, the hide became damaged due to prolonged light exposure, temperature and humidity fluctuations, and confinement in too small a case. In 2010, the hide underwent conservation treatment and is back on display.

Wyoming has long had a rich history in dinosaur fossil discoveries. These are casts of fossils excavated in the late 1990s at the Sheridan College Dinosaur Quarry One on Poison Creek, south of Buffalo. These vertebrae came from the tail of an Allosaurus named "Caesar." Over 1,000 dinosaur bones were excavated, and most are now on display at the St. Paul Science Center in Minnesota.

This is a rare Native American stone bowl, made from steatite. It was discovered at a river crossing on Onion Gulch within the Bighorn National Forest in Wyoming. The bowl was hand carved from a single rock. It measures five inches tall and four and a half inches in diameter.

These Northern Cheyenne medicine rattles are sacred. One black and one white, they are marked with the Camp of Two Moons, and according to tradition, must not be separated. One day, a Cheyenne Indian came into the drugstore and offered the white rattle to Jim Gatchell. Knowing it must have been stolen but not wanting to offend, Gatchell accepted the rattle. Later that day, he offered to return the rattle to some Cheyenne Indians visiting the drugstore. Rather than taking the rattle, the Cheyenne refused, left the store, and returned to present the matching black rattle. The rattles are decorated with horsehair and must face opposite directions when displayed.

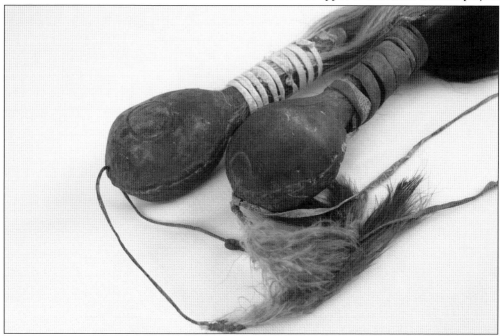

This is a beaded vest from the family of Minnicoujou Lakota Chief Hump II (c. 1848–1908), who participated in the Rosebud Battle, Battle of Little Bighorn, and the Ghost Dance. It was made by one or both of Hump's Cheyenne wives, who were sisters. His father, Chief Hump I, led the charge against Capt. William Fetterman's soldiers outside Fort Phil Kearny in Wyoming Territory on December 21, 1866. Chief Hump II, age 16, was also present at the battle and, with his father, also took part in the Wagon Box, Platte Bridge, and Dull Knife battles. Chief Hump II and his band went to Canada before returning to the United States, among the last Sioux bands to return. They settled on the Cheyenne River Sioux Reservation and maintained the old ways using lodges and traditional clothing. The vest is made from blue, white, and red seed beads. The fringe along the bottom consists of porcupine quillwork, dyed horsehair, and metal bugle beads. It was obtained from the Crow Agency by Col. Archibald Rogers.

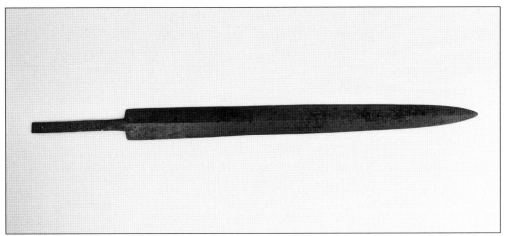

The Sorby company was established in 1790 in Sheffield, England, and made edged tools such as sheep shears, spades, and shovels. When the son of the founder joined the firm in 1827, the "I & H Sorby" mark was adopted. The firm exported its products to trading posts across the British Empire, which is how this lance head made its way to America and was discovered near Fort Caspar, Wyoming.

This is an example of a Southern Arapaho war bonnet. As a nationally accredited museum organized within a local government structure, the museum can house items that include bald eagle feathers, which are federally protected. This headdress is composed of eagle feathers with red thread around the ends attached to the headband. The band features multicolored beads in triangle shapes with a cross in the center.

According to a scholar on Native American history, this is almost certainly a Mountain Crow war shield based on the symbolism depicted. The incoming bullets around the upper circumference of the shield are being repelled by the radiant power of the supernatural protective figure, making the shield invulnerable to firearms. The figure, whose identity is unknown, has lightning blazing from its eyes. The horns on the figure could represent Powers from Below (such as subterranean serpents, bulls, and felines) or could represent an avatar of thunder, which has been depicted wearing the horned scalps of Netherworld powers it has dispatched. Another reason it is believed this shield is Crow is due to how the images were applied. It was characteristic of many Crow shields for the imagery to be generally finger painted and daubed, as opposed to the Cheyenne and Arapaho tribes' practice of outlining the images, then daubing. The feathers attached to the shield are from great horned owls. This shield was part of Jim Gatchell's original collection.

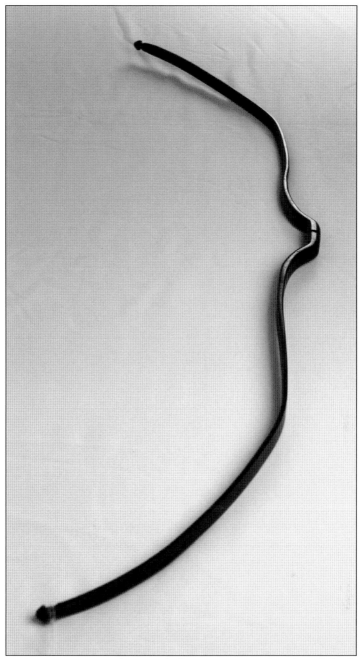

This is a Native American recurve bow made from one piece of steel, with both ends finished with a mushroom-shaped knob, with a deep groove around the base of the knobs. The metal is thickest at the handle and then thins and flattens as the arms extend outwards. There are shallow grooves on two sides of the handle. The curves of the bow measure a total of 44.5 inches in length and 38.625 inches from tip to tip in a straight line. It was found near Upper Prairie Dog Creek (called Peno Creek in 1866) in northern Johnson County. The mystery is that neither Plains Indians nor white settlers were widely known to use steel bows. It was common for Native Americans to find blacksmiths to craft items, and perhaps this bow was one.

Born in Germany in the late 1830s, Adolph Metzger immigrated to Pennsylvania with his family in 1848. He enlisted in the US Army in 1855 and served as a private during the 1857 expedition against the Mormons in Utah and during the American Civil War. Metzger arrived as Fort Phil Kearny's bugler in November 1866 with eight months of duty left to serve. He reportedly fought in hand-to-hand combat using his bugle during the Fetterman Fight on December 21, 1866. The Native Americans noted his tenacity, and as a sign of great respect, honored him by covering his un-mutilated body with a bison hide. Many years after the battle, Metzger's bugle was found and later given to Jim Gatchell to display in his store. In 2016, the bugle was voted the most significant artifact in the state of Wyoming in a contest sponsored by the University of Wyoming Libraries and the Wyoming State Historical Society.

Wood was used to construct fort buildings and provide heat in the winter. Many forts had wood depots and lumber camps within a few miles. This saw blade was manufactured in Ohio and arrived at Fort Phil Kearny in 1866. It would have been used at one of the three steam-powered sawmills near the fort to cut logs and boards to size.

These two J. Browne & Son Company, P & J Arnold Company ink bottles traveled from London, England, to Trabing Crossing, along the Bozeman Trail. The large bottles would have been used to dispense small quantities of ink into receptacles for writing. Based on its location, these bottles were used at Fort Reno, near present-day Kaycee, Wyoming.

This "Wagon Box Fight" diorama was commissioned in 1957 to be installed in the new Jim Gatchell Memorial Museum. The museum paid $3,500 to Denver-based artist Juan Menchaca, who built the diorama components by hand. The diorama depicts the August 2, 1867, Wagon Box Fight where Native Americans attacked two officers, 26 enlisted men, and two civilian teamsters at a wood camp makeshift corral six miles from Fort Phil Kearny.

At the Wagon Box Fight, soldiers and teamsters took shelter behind 14 wagon boxes, which were removed from their running gear and placed in an oval on the ground. They fared better than those at the Fetterman Fight due to their newly issued breech-loading Springfield rifles (like the one pictured), which had a quicker rate of fire. Three soldiers were killed, and several were wounded. The Native American losses are not known.

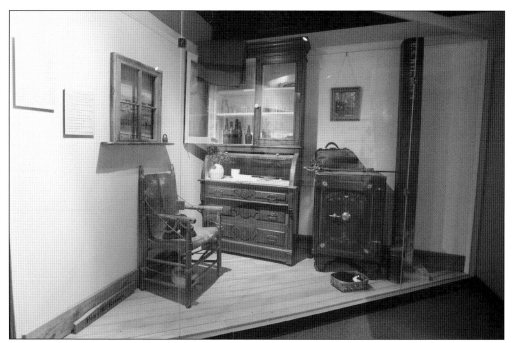

Fort McKinney was moved in the summer of 1878 to the base of the Bighorn Mountains from its original location near old Fort Reno. Until 1894, its function was to discourage off-reservation travel by Native Americans. As it offered jobs and markets, Fort McKinney's presence led to the development of the town of Buffalo. When it was decommissioned, the fort became the Veterans' Home of Wyoming. This photograph shows the Fort McKinney exhibit.

Fort McKinney featured barracks for seven companies of troops and at least 14 structures for officer quarters, stables, warehouses, laundress quarters, a hospital, a bakery, offices, and auxiliary buildings. Several companies of the African American 9th Cavalry were stationed at the fort. Markers such as the one pictured were used to denote the boundaries of the military reservation. Several markers can still be found around Buffalo.

This original Basque sheep wagon, restored in the 1990s, was owned by Martin Pelloux from 1903 to 1919. It was built by the Rice brothers of Florence Hardware in Douglas, Wyoming. These wagons were used by sheepherders while tending their flocks. The sheep wagon contains a small wood stove, bed, small hideaway table, and side benches and cabinets.

Fire hose carts such as this were pulled by firefighters to a fire. At the scene, the hose was unwound from the cart, laid out, and connected to a hand pumper to pump water from a cistern or pond. The narrow metal wheels indicate that this cart was primarily used for paved streets within the city of Buffalo.

This series of paintings by artist Mel Gerhold illustrate the boom years of the cattle industry in the late 1800s through the disastrous winter of 1886–1887, when relentless blizzards killed hundreds of thousands of cattle on the prairie. This catastrophe contributed to the downfall, or bust, of cattle businesses, as well as the Johnson County Cattle War. The panels are designed to be viewed from left to right. The panels, in order, are titled "Spring," "Summer," "Fall," and "Winter." Gerhold was born in 1928 and began his career as a full-time painter in 1949. He specialized in cowboy frontier and Native American genre painting. Most of his artworks were in oil, but he also sculpted and did drawings in both pencil and pen and ink. He generally did not work from photographs unless it was necessary for reference.

"The Siege at the TA Ranch" was another Juan Menchaca diorama commissioned by the museum in 1957. It cost $2,500 and highlights the three-day siege at the TA Ranch between the "Invaders" and Johnson County citizens during the Johnson County Cattle War. The Invaders, alerted that a large force was heading toward them, took refuge at the ranch. Depicted is the "Go-Devil," a defensive structure on wheels that was built to allow the citizens to get close to the Invaders while

being protected from gunfire, like a rolling fort. The running gear from two abandoned wagons were placed side-by-side, and a framework of logs was built. In the scene, the Go-Devil is shown being rolled up to an earthwork trench where some of the Invaders were stationed, just as troops from Fort McKinney's 6th Cavalry arrived.

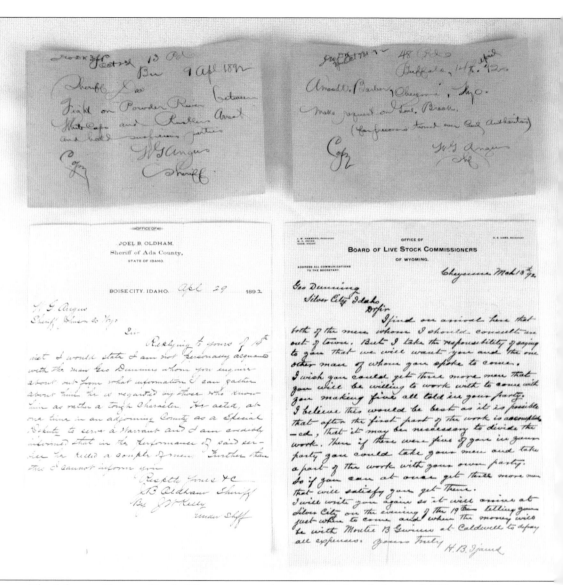

The Johnson County Cattle War was a war between the "cattle barons" (Wyoming Stock Growers Association) and independent ranchers and homesteaders. It was a struggle for power and survival of the Wyoming cattle industry. The WSGA had invested much of the capital into the infrastructure of Wyoming, developing roads, markets, and range management policies. Its dominance in the ranching economy influenced the political and economic spheres of Wyoming Territory. As homesteaders began arriving and putting up fences, conflicts arose as WSGA members lost access to range, water, and grass that they felt they owned. These documents are primary source examples from the William "Red" Angus collection. Angus was the Johnson County sheriff during the war and was considered by the stock growers to be sympathetic to the small ranchers and homesteaders.

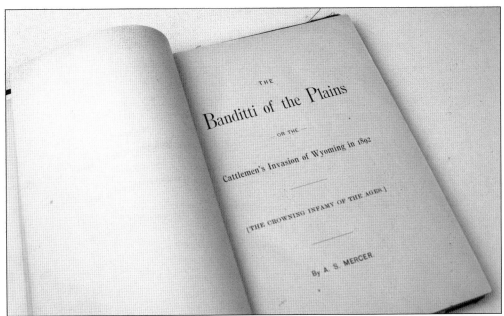

This is a first edition of Asa Mercer's *The Banditti of the Plains*, owned by Red Angus. Asa Mercer came to Wyoming as an editor of the Wyoming Stock Growers Association's *Northwest Livestock Journal*. As the Johnson County Cattle War unfolded in April 1892, Mercer began to sympathize with the Johnson County citizens. After its publication, the WSGA worked to destroy as many copies of the book as possible.

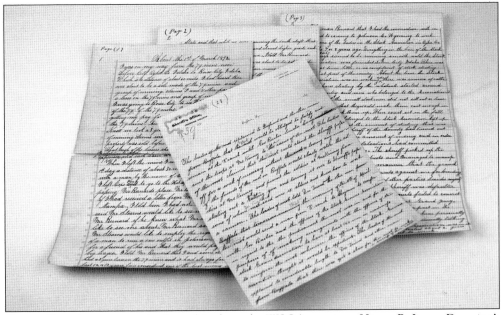

George Dunning was recruited as a hired gun by WSGA secretary Hiram B. Ijams. Dunning's role was to kill "rustlers" and frighten others into leaving the state during the Johnson County Cattle War. He was the only Invader to be incarcerated at the Johnson County jail. There, he wrote his 44-page confession (four pages pictured), exposing the background, participants, and goals of the Invaders.

At the age of 14, Tom Horn left his Missouri home and headed west in 1874 with $11 to his name. Arriving in 1894, Horn worked various jobs throughout Wyoming before becoming known as a stock detective and brand inspector for the WSGA. There is evidence that he killed or threatened several notorious cattle thieves across Wyoming and Colorado. Horn was friends with John Coble, a rancher heavily involved with the WSGA. Coble had a feud with a neighbor, Kels Nickell, that led to one of Kels's sons, Willie Nickell, being shot and killed on July 18, 1901. Horn's reputation as a killer and his friendship with John Coble led him to become a suspect. Horn was arrested after US marshal Joseph LeFors acquired a damaging confession. Horn was tried, convicted, and hanged on November 20, 1903. Pictured are Horn's rifle and spurs from the museum collection.

The Basque country consists of three provinces in France and four in Spain. Geographically and politically divided, when the Basque immigrated to the United States and Wyoming, they held on to their traditions, language, and culture. Music and dance still play a part in sustaining a Basque identity in Buffalo. This accordion was used for many years by Joseph Bilbao at Basque celebrations.

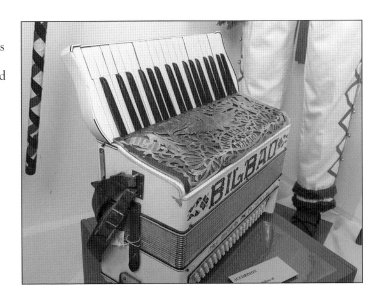

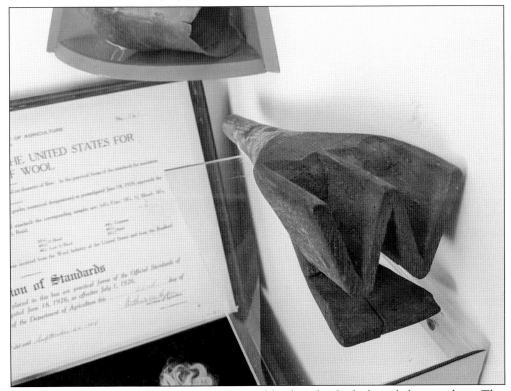

Sheep are paint stamped to allow owners to quickly identify which sheep belong to them. This was important especially when flocks were set loose among pastures in the Powder River region and the summer pastures in the Bighorn Mountains. Once a sheep was sheared, the paint stamp would have to be reapplied. This paint stamp was probably hand-carved by Jean Auzqui and dates to the 1920s.

In 1958, the museum board realized $8,000 remained in the building fund. For $2,500, the third Juan Menchaca diorama, "Main Street, 1884," was ordered. Based on a historic photograph in the museum's collection, it features future US president Theodore Roosevelt and Arthur W. Merrifield, Roosevelt's North Dakota ranch foreman. On two occasions in 1884, Roosevelt visited Buffalo while on hunting expeditions in the Bighorn Mountains. The diorama captures some of the first

businesses in northern Wyoming and the oldest on Buffalo's Main Street: the Stebbins, Conrad, and Company Bank (now First Northern Bank of Wyoming), the Occidental Hotel, and the John H. Conrad and Company Store. The dusty, curving street, the wooden sidewalks, and the freight teams present an accurate depiction of a typical cowtown in 1884.

In 1943, a World War II B-17 aircraft crashed in the Bighorn Mountains. Visitors are still fascinated by the mystery of how the crash occurred. Many items from the crash site are featured in an exhibit at the Jim Gatchell Memorial Museum. The museum is a repository for items that have been removed from the crash since its discovery in 1945. This propeller came from the aircraft.

The B-17 that crashed in the Bighorn Mountains contained a crew of 10 men, who died on impact. They were en route to Grand Island Army Air Base in Nebraska from Pendleton Field in Oregon. When the crash site was discovered in 1945, the plane was 110 miles off course. This lapel pin would have been worn by officers in the US Army Air Force who completed aviation cadet school.

When the B-17 hit the ridge, metal wrinkled like paper, tops of rocks were sheared off, engines were thrown hundreds of yards, and huge pieces of metal were lodged in the boulder field. This .50 caliber machine gun was taken from the crash site and shows extensive damage. Veterans' groups petitioned to have the ridge named in honor of the crew. In 1946, it was officially christened Bomber Mountain.

The Daughters of the American Revolution sponsored a contest in 1917 to design a Wyoming state flag. Buffalo native and artist Verna Keays submitted a drawing and won $20 for her entry. After its official adoption, this silk taffeta, gold-fringed flag with a hand-painted bison and seal was purchased by the state.

The Bighorn National Forest, founded in 1897, is among the oldest of the national forests in the United States. In 2020, the Jim Gatchell Memorial Museum became the repository of over 100 years of historical records pertaining to the Bighorns. This photograph is part of the over 10,000 documents, maps, brochures, environmental impact studies, grazing permits, field notebooks, letters, photographs, and more that make up this collection.

This 1873 Springfield rifle is from Jim Gatchell's original collection. Gifted by Cheyenne warrior Shave Head, the rifle was picked up as a spoil of war at the Battle of the Little Bighorn. Gatchell considered it the most valuable item in his collection. It was later ascertained during conservation maintenance in the 1990s that although found at the site, the rifle was not used during the battle.

This is the two-room, 16-by-32-foot Jenkins Homestead cabin. It was built by Marshall Jenkins north-northeast of Kaycee, Wyoming, in 1915. The Jenkins family dry-farmed there while raising the first three of their eight children until 1923, when the cabin was sold. Decades later, daughter Polly bought and relocated the cabin to Story, Wyoming, and eventually donated it to the museum in 2006.

The Jim Gatchell Memorial Museum's interpretive tipi features artwork from two Native American artists: Northern Cheyenne Bilford Curley Sr. and Lakota James Starkey. The artwork depicts Cheyenne and Lakota warriors meeting at the tipi, which forms the tail of a multi-colored water bird. The clouds are raining soldiers, while the Lakota side illustrates glimpses of friends and heroes such as Spotted Wolf and the Girl Who Saved Her Brother.

D. Michael Thomas is an award-winning local artist who sculpts Western bronzes, focusing on historical and western life. Thomas's work is prominent throughout Buffalo and Johnson County with multiple public displays. *The Coats of Winter* sculpture pictured here features a team of horses pulling a hay wagon with a cowboy and dog.

During the Johnson County Cattle War, while staying at the KC Cabin, Nate Champion single-handedly held the Invaders at bay for hours, allowing witnesses to discover the invasion and get the news to Buffalo. This D. Michael Thomas statue depicts the moment when Champion ran from the burning cabin before being shot down. His actions allowed Johnson County citizens to confront the Invaders at the TA Ranch.

These hand-stamped metal tags were the first numbering system used by Jim Gatchell to identify and inventory his historic items, which became the nucleus of the Jim Gatchell Memorial Museum. Seen in photographs of Gatchell in the drugstore, we know that he saw the value of recording his collection. His original collection included some 150 firearms (90 rifles or rifle pieces, 25 shotguns, and 35 pistols); 42 sabers, swords, or bayonets; 36 single or groups of arrowheads; 4 bows; 4 pairs of moccasins; and 2 war bonnets. Today, the museum has processed over 42,000 items. Most recent acquisitions include a Crow Indian tipi, displayed outside with the museum's Northern Cheyenne tipi, and seven pieces of original artwork from Neltje, an abstract expressionist painter, artist, and author who lived near Buffalo in Banner, Wyoming. She painted acrylics, monotypes, and mixed media and with a sumi-e brush.

DISCOVER THOUSANDS OF LOCAL HISTORY BOOKS FEATURING MILLIONS OF VINTAGE IMAGES

Arcadia Publishing, the leading local history publisher in the United States, is committed to making history accessible and meaningful through publishing books that celebrate and preserve the heritage of America's people and places.

Find more books like this at
www.arcadiapublishing.com

Search for your hometown history, your old stomping grounds, and even your favorite sports team.

Consistent with our mission to preserve history on a local level, this book was printed in South Carolina on American-made paper and manufactured entirely in the United States. Products carrying the accredited Forest Stewardship Council (FSC) label are printed on 100 percent FSC-certified paper.

MADE IN THE USA